Pebble® Plus

## Under the Sea
# Clown Fish

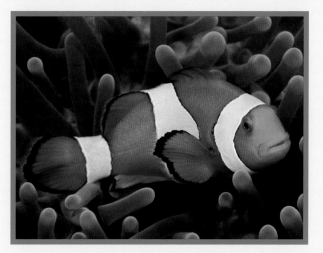

by Carol K. Lindeen

Consulting Editor: Gail Saunders-Smith, PhD

Consultant: Jody Rake, Member
Southwest Marine/Aquatic Educator's Association

Capstone
press
Mankato, Minnesota

Pebble Plus is published by Capstone Press,
1710 Roe Crest Drive, North Mankato, Minnesota 56003.
www.capstonepub.com

*Library of Congress Cataloging-in-Publication Data*
Lindeen, Carol K., 1976–
    Clown fish / by Carol K. Lindeen.
    p. cm.—(Pebble plus: Under the sea)
    Includes bibliographical references (p. 23) and index.
    ISBN-13: 978-0-7368-2598-6 (hardcover)
    ISBN-10: 0-7368-2598-3 (hardcover)
    ISBN-13: 978-0-7368-5110-7 (paperback)
    ISBN-10: 0-7368-5110-0 (paperback)
    1. Clown anemonefish—Juvenile literature. [1. Clown anemonefish. 2. Fishes.] I. Title.
QL638.P77L56 2005
597'.72—dc22                                                    2003025608

Summary: Simple text and photographs present the lives of clown fish.

**Editorial Credits**
Martha E. H. Rustad, editor; Juliette Peters, designer; Kelly Garvin, photo researcher;
    Karen Hieb, product planning editor

**Photo Credits**
Bruce Coleman Inc./Carl Roessler, 12–13
Corbis/Amos Nachoum, cover; Chase Swift, 21
Jeff Rotman, 14–15, 16–17
Minden Pictures/Chris Newbert, 4–5
PhotoDisc Inc./Frank & Joyce Burek, 1
Seapics.com/Franco Banfi, 6–7; Kevin Palmer, 8–9; Mark Conlin, 10–11; Marc Bernardi, 18–19

## Note to Parents and Teachers

The Under the Sea series supports national science standards related to the diversity
and unity of life. This book describes and illustrates clown fish. The images support
early readers in understanding the text. The repetition of words and phrases helps early
readers learn new words. This book also introduces early readers to subject-specific
vocabulary words, which are defined in the Glossary section. Early readers may need
assistance to read some words and to use the Table of Contents, Glossary, Read More,
Internet Sites, and Index/Word List sections of the book.

**Word Count: 123**
**Early-Intervention Level: 15**

Printed in the United States of America in North Mankato, Minnesota.
072014     008321R

# Table of Contents

# Clown Fish

What are clown fish?
Clown fish are
brightly colored fish.

Clown fish have orange
bodies with stripes.
Clown fish are about
as big as a person's hand.

Clown fish use
their fins to swim.

Clown fish swim with many other animals near coral reefs.

# Living with Sea Anemones

Clown fish live with sea anemones in coral reefs. Sea anemones are animals that look like flowers.

Sea anemones sting and
kill fish. But the stings
do not hurt clown fish.
A layer of slime on their
scales protects clown fish.

Clown fish and sea anemones
help each other. Clown fish
stay safe by swimming near
sea anemones.

Clown fish eat food that
sea anemones leave
behind. This helps keep
sea anemones clean.

# Under the Sea

Clown fish swim
under the sea.

# Glossary

coral reef—a type of land made up of the hardened skeletons of corals; corals are small, colorful sea creatures.

fin—a thin body part on a swimming animal; fins help fish swim and move in the water.

reef—an underwater strip of rocks, coral, or sand near the surface of the ocean

scale—one of the small, thin plates that covers the bodies of fish

sea anemone—a sea animal with a tube-shaped body and many tentacles

slime—a soft, slippery substance

sting—to hurt with a sharp, venomous tip; sea anemones sting fish and other sea animals, but clown fish are not hurt by their stings.

# Read More

**Galko, Francine.** *Coral Reef Animals.* Animals in Their Habitats. Chicago: Heinemann Library, 2003.

**Schaefer, Lola M.** *Sea Anemones.* Ooey-Gooey Animals. Chicago: Heinemann Library, 2002.

**Stille, Darlene R.** *I Am a Fish: The Life of a Clown Fish.* I Live in the Ocean. Minneapolis: Picture Window Books, 2004.

# Internet Sites

FactHound offers a safe, fun way to find Internet sites related to this book. All of the sites on FactHound have been researched by our staff.

Here's how:

1. Visit *www.facthound.com*

2. Type in this special code **0736825983** for age-appropriate sites. Or enter a search word related to this book for a more general search.

3. Click on the **Fetch It** button.

FactHound will fetch the best sites for you!

# Index/Word List